Kaplan Publishing are constantly finding ways to make a difference to your studies and our exciting online resources really do offer something different to students looking for exam success.

This book comes with free MyKaplan online resources so that you can study anytime, anywhere. **This free online resource is not sold separately and is included in the price of the book.**

Having purchased this book, you have access to the following online study materials:

CONTENT	AAT	
	Text	Kit
iPaper version of the book	✓	✓
Progress tests with instant answers	✓	
Mock assessments online	✓	✓
Material updates	✓	✓

How to access your online resources

Kaplan Financial students will already have a MyKaplan account and these extra resources will be available to you online. You do not need to register again, as this process was completed when you enrolled. If you are having problems accessing online materials, please ask your course administrator.

If you are already a registered MyKaplan user go to www.MyKaplan.co.uk and log in. Select the 'add a book' feature and enter the ISBN number of this book and the unique pass key at the bottom of this card. Then click 'finished' or 'add another book'. You may add as many books as you have purchased from this screen.

If you purchased through Kaplan Flexible Learning or via the Kaplan Publishing website you will automatically receive an e-mail invitation to MyKaplan. Please register your details using this email to gain access to your content. If you do not receive the e-mail or book content, please contact Kaplan Flexible Learning.

If you are a new user register at www.MyKaplan.co.uk and click on the link contained in the email we sent you to activate your account. Then select the 'add a book' feature, enter the ISBN number of this book and the unique pass key at the bottom of this card. Then click 'finished' or 'add another book'.

Your Code and Information

This code can only be used once for the registration of one book online. This registration and your online content will expire when the final sittings for the examinations covered by this book have taken place. Please allow one hour from the time you submit your book details for us to process your request.

Please scratch the film to access your MyKaplan code.

TLFb-DZAO-wQD2-yJCt

Please be aware that this code is case-sensitive and you will need to include the dashes within the passcode, but not when entering the ISBN. For further technical support, please visit www.MyKaplan.co.uk

Professional Examinations

AQ2013 Level 2

Processing Bookkeeping Transactions

REVISION KIT

British Library Cataloguing-in-Publication Data

A catalogue record for this book is available from the British Library.

Published by:

Kaplan Publishing UK

Unit 2 The Business Centre

Molly Millar's Lane

Wokingham

Berkshire

RG41 2QZ

ISBN: 978-1-78415-351-9

© Kaplan Financial Limited, 2015

Printed and bound in Great Britain.

CONTENTS

Features in this exam kit

In addition to providing a wide ranging bank of real exam style questions, we have also included in this kit:

- Paper specific information and advice on exam technique.

- Our recommended approach to make your revision for this particular subject as effective as possible.

You will find a wealth of other resources to help you with your studies on the AAT website:

www.mykaplan.co.uk

www.aat.org.uk/

Quality and accuracy are of the utmost importance to us so if you spot an error in any of our products, please send an email to mykaplanreporting@kaplan.com with full details, or follow the link to the feedback form in MyKaplan.

Our Quality Co-ordinator will work with our technical team to verify the error and take action to ensure it is corrected in future editions.

INDEX TO QUESTIONS AND ANSWERS

EXAM TECHNIQUE

- **Do not skip any of the material** in the syllabus.

- **Read each question** *very* carefully.

- **Double-check your answer** before committing yourself to it.

- Answer **every** question – if you do not know an answer to a multiple choice question or true/false question, you don't lose anything by guessing. Think carefully before you **guess**.

- If you are answering a multiple-choice question, **eliminate first those answers that you know are wrong**. Then choose the most appropriate answer from those that are left.

Computer-based exams – tips

- Do not attempt a CBA until you have **completed all study material** relating to it.

- On the AAT website there is a CBA demonstration. It is **ESSENTIAL** that you attempt this before your real CBA. You will become familiar with how to move around the CBA screens and the way that questions are formatted, increasing your confidence and speed in the actual exam.

- Be sure you understand how to use the **software** before you start the exam. If in doubt, ask the assessment centre staff to explain it to you.

- Questions are **displayed on the screen** and answers are entered using keyboard and mouse. At the end of the exam, you are given a certificate showing the result you have achieved.

- In addition to the traditional multiple-choice question type, CBAs will also contain **other types of questions**, such as number entry questions, drag and drop, true/false, pick lists or drop down menus or hybrids of these.

- In some CBAs you will have to type in complete computations or written answers.

- You need to be sure you **know how to answer questions** of this type before you sit the exam, through practice.

PAPER SPECIFIC INFORMATION

THE ASSESSMENT

FORMAT OF THE ASSESSMENT

The assessment consists of ten tasks in one section.

The task content is outlined below.

Task	Maximum marks	Title for topics within task range
1	15	Making entries in an analysed day book
2	15	Transferring data from day books to ledgers
3	20	Make entries in a three column cash book
4	15	Transfer data from a three column cash book
5	20	Make entries in and transfers from an analysed petty cash book
6	20	Prepare an initial trial balance
7	15	Check supplier invoices/credit notes
8	15	Prepare sales invoice or credit note, Check the accuracy of receipts from customers
9	15	Prepare a statement of account from an account in the sales ledger
10	15	Understanding the double entry system

Sales and purchases day-books and sales and purchases returns day-books

Students will be required to make entries in at least one day-book; that is sales, sales returns,

purchases and purchases returns day-books, using given data or source documents. The day-books will include net, VAT, gross and analytical columns and one for customer or supplier account codes.

Students will also be required to transfer data from at least one of the day-books listed above to the sales or purchases ledger and general ledger.

Three column analysed cash-book

Students will be required to make entries into one or both sides of the cash-book using given data or source documents reflecting different methods of payment, For example, cash, cheques and

automated payments. Numerical columns could include cash, bank, discounts, VAT, trade receivables, trade payables, cash sales, cash purchases, income and expenses.

Students should be prepared to total the columns and balance the cash-book or answer questions on the cash and bank balances.

Students will also be required to transfer data from the cash-book to the sales, purchases and general ledgers. They must understand that the cash-book can be a book of prime entry and part of the double entry bookkeeping system or a book of prime entry alone.

Petty cash-book

Students should be prepared to make entries for payments and the reimbursement of petty cash in an analysed petty-cash book from given data or source documents and to identify the subsequent entries in the general ledger. Students should be prepared to total the columns and balance the petty cashbook. They must understand the imprest system, and that the petty cash-book can be a book of prime entry and part of the double entry bookkeeping system or a book of prime entry alone.

Students will be asked to conduct a simple reconciliation of the cash in hand with the petty cash-book balance, which may involve calculating the individual and total amounts of notes and coins from a given list.

Whilst students will not be asked to prepare a petty cash voucher, they should be able to identify the purpose and content of a petty cash voucher.

Understanding coding within a double entry bookkeeping system

As well as entering codes in the sales and purchases and returns day-books, students will be required to understand the function of coding. Codes include customer and supplier account codes, general ledger codes and product codes. Students may be required to create codes that are consistent with the organisation's coding policy. They may also be asked to enter codes when preparing sales invoices and credit notes.

Double entry bookkeeping

Students should be prepared to answer questions relating to processing transactions throughout the double entry system from books of prime entry to ledgers. Tasks may include questions or

calculations relating to the accounting equation and the dual effect of transactions. Students should be able to define capital and revenue income and expenditure as well as classify such transactions. They should also be able to classify assets or liability accounts.

It is important that students learn how to balance T accounts, clearly showing the totals of each side of the account and the balance carried down and brought down.

Trial balance

Students will be asked to transfer given account balances to the appropriate column of an initial trial balance and total both columns. The trial balance may be in alphabetical or random order, or may follow the structure of final accounts.

Trade, bulk and settlement discounts

Students will need to be able to explain and calculate trade, bulk and settlement discounts together with the appropriate VAT amount. They may be asked to produce a sales invoice or credit note including some or all of these discounts or identify discrepancies in receipts from customers involving incorrect discounts taken. They should also be able to check discounts, and identify discrepancies, on invoices and credit notes from suppliers.

Document preparation and checking

Students must understand the purpose and content of petty cash vouchers, remittance advice notes, sales and purchases invoices and credit notes and statements of account to be sent to customers. They must also be able to prepare and code sales invoices and credit notes, including VAT and trade, bulk and settlement discounts, referring to quotations, discount policy, customer orders, delivery notes and price lists as source documents. They should also be able to prepare statements of account with varying formats.

Students must also be able to check the accuracy of receipts from customers by referring to sales invoices, remittance advice notes and the sales ledger and be able to identify discrepancies for example, under or over payment or incorrect discount taken. They should be aware of the different methods organisations use to make and receive payments.

Students must be able to use purchase orders, goods received notes and delivery notes to check the accuracy of invoices and credit notes from suppliers and identify discrepancies such as non-delivery of goods, incorrect type or quantity of goods, incorrect calculations and incorrect discounts. They must be able to reconcile statements from suppliers with the purchases ledger account and calculate payments due from given data and source documents.

Time allowed

120 minutes (2 hours)

PASS MARK

The pass mark for all AAT CBAs is 70%.

Always keep your eye on the clock and make sure you attempt all questions!

TERMINOLOGY

The AAT fully adopted IFRS terminology on 1 January 2012. The IFRS terms do not impact greatly on Processing Bookkeeping Transactions. The listing provided gives the IFRS term (AAT preferred term) and the related UK GAAP term. You should ensure you are familiar with the following terms:

UK GAAP	IFRS
Trade debtors/Debtors	Trade receivables/Receivables
Trade creditors/Creditors	Trade payables/Payables
Debtors ledger control account	Receivables ledger control account
Sales ledger control account	Sales ledger control account
Creditors ledger control account	Payables ledger control account
Purchases ledger control account	Purchases ledger control account
Sales/Purchases ledger	Sales/Purchases ledger
Sales tax/VAT	Sales tax/VAT
Fixed asset	Non-current asset
Stock	Inventory
Bad debt	Irrecoverable debt

DETAILED SYLLABUS

The detailed syllabus and study guide written by the AAT can be found at:

www.aat.org.uk/

KAPLAN PUBLISHING

KAPLAN'S RECOMMENDED REVISION APPROACH

QUESTION PRACTICE IS THE KEY TO SUCCESS

Success in professional examinations relies upon you acquiring a firm grasp of the required knowledge at the tuition phase. In order to be able to do the questions, knowledge is essential.

However, the difference between success and failure often hinges on your exam technique on the day and making the most of the revision phase of your studies.

The Kaplan textbook is the starting point, designed to provide the underpinning knowledge to tackle all questions. However, in the revision phase, poring over text books is not the answer.

The Kaplan workbook helps you consolidate your knowledge and understanding and is a useful tool to check whether you can remember key topic areas.

Kaplan pocket notes are designed to help you quickly revise a topic area; however you then need to practise questions. There is a need to progress to exam style questions as soon as possible, and to tie your exam technique and technical knowledge together.

The importance of question practice cannot be over-emphasised.

The recommended approach below is designed by expert tutors in the field, in conjunction with their knowledge of the examiner and the specimen assessment.

You need to practise as many questions as possible in the time you have left.

OUR AIM

Our aim is to get you to the stage where you can attempt exam questions confidently, to time, in a closed book environment, with no supplementary help (i.e. to simulate the real examination experience).

Practising your exam technique is also vitally important for you to assess your progress and identify areas of weakness that may need more attention in the final run up to the examination.

In order to achieve this we recognise that initially you may feel the need to practise some questions with open book help.

Good exam technique is vital.

THE KAPLAN PBKT REVISION PLAN

Stage 1: Assess areas of strengths and weaknesses

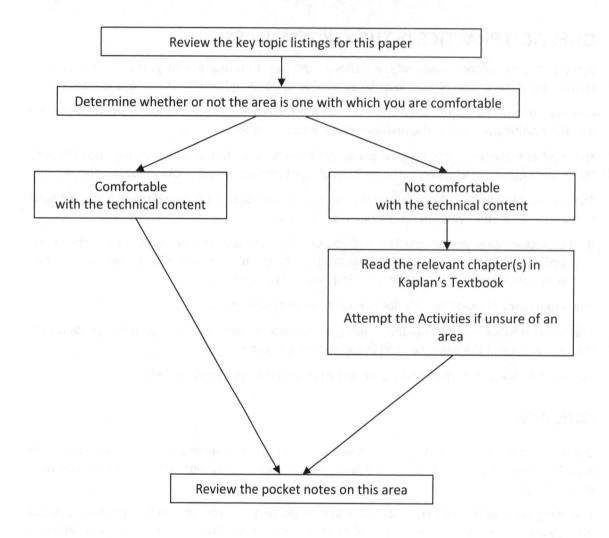

Stage 2: Practice questions

Follow the order of revision of topics as presented in this kit and attempt the questions in the order suggested.

Try to avoid referring to text books and notes and the model answer until you have completed your attempt.

Review your attempt with the model answer and assess how much of the answer you achieved.

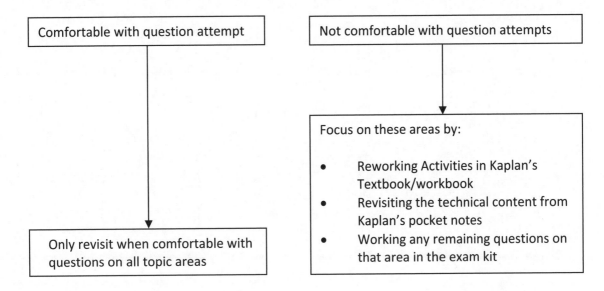

Stage 3: Final pre-exam revision

We recommend that you **attempt at least one mock examination** containing a set of previously unseen exam standard questions.

Attempt the mock CBA online in timed, closed book conditions to simulate the real exam experience

Section 2

ANSWERS TO PRACTICE QUESTIONS

MAKING ENTRIES IN AN ANALYSED DAY BOOK

1   SDB

Sales day-book

Date 20XX	Details	Invoice number	Total £	VAT £	Net £	Sales type 1 £	Sales type 2 £
31 Dec	Poonams	105	3,600	600	3,000		3,000
31 Dec	D. Taylor	106	7,680	1,280	6,400	6,400	
31 Dec	Smiths	107	3,840	640	3,200		3,200
	Totals		15,120	2,520	12,600	6,400	6,200

2   FREDDIE LTD

Purchases day-book

Date 20XX	Details	Invoice number	Total £	VAT £	Net £	Product 14211 £	Product 14212 £
31 July	Box Ltd	2177	960	160	800	800	
31 July	Shrew Ltd	2175	14,400	2,400	12,000	12,000	
31 July	Novot & Co	2176	4,800	800	4,000		4,000
	Totals		20,160	3,360	16,800	12,800	4,000

3   MAHINDRA LTD

Sales day-book

Date 20XX	Details	Invoice number	Total £	VAT £	Net £	Sales type 1 £	Sales type 2 £
31 Jan	Square Ltd	3567	1,200	200	1,000	1,000	
31 Jan	Oval & Co	3568	9,600	1,600	8,000		8,000
31 Jan	Diamond Ltd	3569	13,200	2,200	11,000		11,000
31 Jan	Triangle Ltd	3570	7,920	1,320	6,600	6,600	
	Totals		31,920	5,320	26,600	7,600	19,000

CODING

4   LEO LTD

(a)

General ledger code	GL530
Supplier account code	DEF14

(b)   *CUSTOMER*

To help trace orders and amounts due from particular customers

5   ELLA'S PAINTS

(a)

General ledger code	GL395
Supplier account code	MEG20

(b)

To help trace orders and amounts due to particular suppliers

6   ROBERTO & CO

(a)

Supplier account code	ALE1
General ledger code	GL72

(b)

To help calculate expense incurred in a GL account

TRANSFERRING DATA FROM DAY BOOKS TO LEDGERS

7   LADY LTD

General ledger

Purchases ledger control account

	£			£
		1 Dec Balance b/d		5,103.90
		18 Dec Purchases & Vat		**903.23**

VAT account

	£			£
		1 Dec Balance b/d		526.90
18 Dec PLCA	**150.53**			

DR   **Purchases account**

	£		£
1 Dec Balance b/d	22,379.52		
18 Dec PLCA	**752.70**		

Subsidiary ledger

M Brown

	£		£
		1 Dec Balance b/d	68.50
		1 Dec PDB	**300.00**

H Madden

	£		£
		1 Dec Balance b/d	286.97
		5 Dec PDB	**183.55**

L Singh

	£		£
		1 Dec Balance b/d	125.89
		7 Dec PDB	**132.60**

A Stevens

	£		£
		1 Dec Balance b/d	12.36
		10 Dec PDB	**90.00**

N Shema

	£		£
		1 Dec Balance b/d	168.70
		18 Dec PDB	**197.08**

8   BUTTONS LTD

(a)   What will be the entries in the purchases ledger?

Account name	Amount £	Debit ✔	Credit ✔
Peak & Co	6,240		✔
Max Ltd	12,720		✔
McIntyre Wholesale	5,760		✔
Pigmy Ltd	3,744		✔

(b)   What will be the entries in the general ledger?

Account name	Amount £	Debit ✔	Credit ✔
Purchases	23,720	✔	
VAT	4,744	✔	
Purchase ledger control	28,464		✔

9   SPARKY LTD

(a)   What will be the entries in the sales ledger?

Sales ledger

Account name	Amount £	Debit ✔	Credit ✔
Clarkson Ltd	1,680		✔
Kyle & Co	720		✔

(b)   What will be the entries in the general ledger?

General ledger

Account name	Amount £	Debit ✔	Credit ✔
Sales ledger control account	2,400		✔
Sales returns	2,000	✔	
VAT	400	✔	

10 LOUIS LTD

(a) What will be the entries in the sales ledger?

Account name	Amount £	Debit ✔	Credit ✔
Sheep & Co	3,840	✔	
Cow Ltd	11,760	✔	
Chicken & Partners	6,720	✔	
Pig Ltd	14,496	✔	

(b) What will be the entries in the general ledger?

Account name	Amount £	Debit ✔	Credit ✔
Sales ledger control	36,816	✔	
VAT	6,136		✔
Sales	30,680		✔

11 THOMAS & TILLY

(a) What will be the entries in the purchase ledger?

Purchases ledger

Account name	Amount £	Debit ✔	Credit ✔
May Ltd	1,920	✔	
Hammond & Co	1,200	✔	

(b) What will be the entries in the general ledger?

General ledger

Account name	Amount £	Debit ✔	Credit ✔
Purchase ledger control account	3,120	✔	
Purchase returns	2,600		✔
VAT	520		✔

12   FINCH'S

(a)   What will be the entries in the sales ledger?

Account name	Amount £	Debit ✔	Credit ✔
Lou and Phil's	5,040	✔	
Eddie and Co	10,560	✔	
Noah's Arc	2,880	✔	
Alex and Freddie	720	✔	

(b)   What will be the entries in the general ledger?

Account name	Amount £	Debit ✔	Credit ✔
Sales	16,000		✔
VAT	3,200		✔
Sales ledger control	19,200	✔	

13   JESSICA & CO

(a)   What will be the entries in the purchases ledger?

Purchases ledger

Account name	Amount £	Debit ✔	Credit ✔
Iona Ltd	1,680	✔	
Matilda Ltd	4,320	✔	

(b)   What will be the entries in the general ledger?

General ledger

Account name	Amount £	Debit ✔	Credit ✔
Purchases ledger control account	6,000	✔	
Purchases returns	5,000		✔
VAT	1,000		✔

THE CASH BOOK

14   ABC LTD

(a)   Cash-book – credit side

PLC

Details	Discount	Cash	Bank	VAT	Payables	Cash purchases	Repairs and renewals
Balance b/f							
S. Lampard		216		36		180	
S. Bobbins		264		44		220	
Penny Rhodes		530				530	
Henley's Ltd	125		4,925		4,925		
Epic Equipment Maintenance			480	80			400
Total	125	1,010	5,405	160	4,925	930	400

(b)   Cash book – debit side

ASSETS

Details	Discount	Cash	Bank	Receivables
Balance b/f		1,550	7,425	
D. Davies			851	851
E. Denholm	25		450	450
Total	25	1,550	8,726	1,301

(c)   £540

(d)   £3,321

(e)   Debit

15   BEDS

(a)   Cash-book – credit side

Details	Discount	Cash	Bank	VAT	Payables	Cash purchases	Repairs and renewals
Balance b/f							
A. Blighty Ltd		708		118		590	
R Bromby		228		38		190	
Roxy Bland		230				230	
Burgess Ltd	60		2,400		2,400		
Fast Equipment Repairs			96	16			80
Total	60	1,166	2,496	172	2,400	1,010	80

(b)   **Cash book – debit side**

Details	Discount	Cash	Bank	Receivables
Balance b/f		1,175	3,825	
A Barnett			698	698
H Connelly	22		250	250
Total	22	1,175	4,773	948

(c)   £9

(d)   £2,277

(e)   Debit

16   JO'S

(a)

Details	Discount	Cash	Bank	VAT	Payables	Cash purchases	Stationery expenses
Bal b/f			19,546				
T. Hunkin Ltd		48		8		40	
Victoria Green		96		16		80	
B. Head Ltd		455				455	
Smiths Ltd	250		4,250		4,250		
Arrow Valley Motor Repairs			120	20			100
Total	250	599	23,916	44	4,250	575	100

(b)

Details	Discount	Cash	Bank	Receivables
Balance b/f		986		
J Drummond			623	623
N Atkinson	45		425	425
Total	45	986	1,048	1,048

(c)   £387

(d)   £22,868

(e)   Credit

17   CHUGGER LTD

(a)   **General ledger**

Account name	Amount £	Debit ✔	Credit ✔
Stationery expense	80	✔	
Repairs	200	✔	
VAT	56	✔	

(b)   **Sales ledger**

Account name	Amount £	Debit ✔	Credit ✔
BBG Ltd	7,200		✔
BBG Ltd	180		✔
EFG Ltd	5,000		✔

(c)   **General ledger**

Account name	Amount £	Debit ✔	Credit ✔
Discounts allowed	180	✔	
Sales ledger control	12,200		✔
Sales ledger control	180		✔

18   ITALIAN STALLIONS

(a)   **General ledger**

Account name	Amount £	Debit ✔	Credit ✔
Office supplies	80	✔	
Repairs	160	✔	
VAT	48	✔	

(b)   **Sales ledger**

Account name	Amount £	Debit ✔	Credit ✔
AAG Ltd	4,000		✔
AAG Ltd	250		✔
HLG Ltd	3,000		✔
HLG Ltd	150		✔

(c)   **General ledger**

Account name	Amount £	Debit ✔	Credit ✔
Discounts allowed	400	✔	
Sales ledger control	7,000		✔
Sales ledger control	400		✔

19   FRED'S FISH

(a)   **Sales ledger**

Account name	Amount £	Debit ✔	Credit ✔
K and D Ltd	8,200		✔
K and D Ltd	400		✔

(b)   **General ledger**

Account name	Amount £	Debit ✔	Credit ✔
Discounts allowed	400	✔	
Sales ledger control	8,200		✔
Sales ledger control	400		✔

(c)   **General ledger**

Account name	Amount £	Debit ✔	Credit ✔
Stationery	100	✔	
VAT	20	✔	
Postage	800	✔	

PETTY CASH

20   HICKORY HOUSE

General ledger

Account name	Amount £	Debit ✔	Credit ✔
VAT	6.80	✔	
Postage	15.00	✔	
Motor expenses	12.40	✔	
Office expenses	21.60	✔	
Bank	90		✔

21   MESSI & CO

General ledger

Account name	Amount £	Debit ✔	Credit ✔
VAT	7.25	✔	
Postage	4.50	✔	
Motor expenses	8.00	✔	
Office expenses	28.28	✔	
Petty cash control	48.03		✔

22   STAVROS

General ledger

Account name	Amount £	Debit ✔	Credit ✔
VAT	18.86	✔	
Postage	16.00	✔	
Business travel	30.80	✔	
Sundry expenses	63.50	✔	
Bank	110.00		✔

23   YUMMY CUPCAKES

General ledger

Account name	Amount £	Debit ✔	Credit ✔
VAT	11.07	✔	
Sundry expenses	10.00	✔	
Business travel	45.37	✔	
Postage	4.00	✔	
Petty cash control	70.44		✔

24   OOH LA!

General ledger

Account name	Amount £	Debit ✔	Credit ✔
VAT	15.21	✔	
Postage	36.30	✔	
Sundry expenses	35.05	✔	
Motor expenses	17.00	✔	
Bank	70.00		✔

25   QUEEN VIC

(a)

Amount in petty cash box	**£141.00**
Balance on petty cash account	**£145.00**
Difference	**£4.00**

(b)

Petty cash reimbursement	
Date: 31.07.20XX	
Amount required to restore the cash in the petty cash box.	**£122.75**

26   THE ARCHES

(a) – (b)

Petty cash-book

Debit side		Credit side					
Details	Amount £	Details	Amount £	VAT £	Postage £	Travel £	Stationery £
Balance b/f	200.00	Mick's Motors	20.00			20.00	
		Stamps	19.00		19.00		
		Office Essentials	26.40	4.40			22.00
		Balance c/d	134.60				
	200.00		200.00	4.40	19.00	20.00	22.00

27   RAINBOW

(a) – (b)

Petty cash-book

Debit side		Credit side					
Details	Amount £	Details	Amount £	VAT £	Postage £	Travel £	Stationery £
Balance b/f	100.00	Colin's Cabs	28.00			28.00	
		Post Office	18.00		18.00		
		ABC Stationery	38.40	6.40			32.00
		Balance c/d	15.60				
	100.00		100.00	6.40	18.00	28.00	32.00

28   SOOTY & SWEEP

(a)

Amount in petty cash box	**£127.40**
Balance on petty cash account	**£135.00**
Difference	**£7.60**

(b)

Petty cash reimbursement	
Date: 31.07.20XX	
Amount required to restore the cash in the petty cash box.	**£245.00**

29 JAWS DENTISTRY

(a) – (b)

Petty cash-book

Debit side		Credit side					
Details	Amount £	Details	Amount £	VAT £	Postage £	Travel £	Stationery £
Balance b/f	225.00	Ace Taxis	26.00			26.00	
		Kate's Couriers	27.00		27.00		
		Smiths Stationery	45.60	7.60			38.00
		Balance c/d	126.40				
	225.00		**225.00**	**7.60**	**27.00**	**26.00**	**38.00**

30 TOM'S TILES

(a)

Amount in petty cash box	**£162.12**
Balance on petty cash account	**£165.52**
Difference	**£3.40**

(b)

Petty cash reimbursement	
Date: 30.04.20XX	
Amount required to restore the cash in petty cash box	**£224.12**

31 ROCKY RILEY

(a) – (b)

Petty cash-book

Debit side		Credit side					
Details	Amount £	Details	Amount £	VAT £	Postage £	Travel £	Stationery £
Balance b/f	175.00	Kath's Kars	32.00			32.00	
		Stamps	25.00		25.00		
		Pauline's Pens	24.00	4.00			20.00
		Balance c/d	94.00				
	175.00		175.00	4.00	25.00	32.00	20.00

32   MHAIRI MOTORS

(a)

Amount in petty cash box	**£99.80**
Balance on petty cash account	**£110.00**
Difference	**£10.20**

(b)

Petty cash reimbursement	
Date: 31.07.20XX	
Amount required to restore the cash in the petty cash box.	**£191.50**

DRAFTING AN INITIAL TRIAL BALANCE

33   BROOKLYN BOATS

Telephone

Date 20XX	Details	Amount £	Date 20XX	Details	Amount £
01 Dec	Balance b/f	870	31 Dec	Balance c/d	1,220
12 Dec	Bank	350			
	Total	1,220		**Total**	1,220
1 Jan	Balance b/d	1,220			

Discounts received

Date 20XX	Details	Amount £	Date 20XX	Details	Amount £
31 Dec	Balance c/d	600	1 Dec	Balance b/f	500
			15 Dec	Purchase Ledger control	100
	Total	600		**Total**	600
			1 Jan	Balance b/d	600

34   WIGGLE POGGLE LTD

Discount allowed

Date 20XX	Details	Amount £	Date 20XX	Details	Amount £
01 July	Balance b/f	1,560	31 July	Balance c/d	2,160
14 July	Sales ledger control account (SLCA)	480			
		120			
	Sales ledger control account (SLCA)				
	Total	2,160		**Total**	2,160
1 Aug	Balance b/d	2,160			

Interest income

Date 20XX	Details	Amount £	Date 20XX	Details	Amount £
31 July	Balance c/d	400	01 July	Balance b/f	320
			28 July	Bank	80
	Total	400		**Total**	400
			1 Aug	Balance b/d	400

35   CRAZY CURTAINS

Electricity expense

Date 20XX	Details	Amount £	Date 20XX	Details	Amount £
01 Jan	Bal b/f	200	31 Jan	Balance c/d	450
22 Jan	Bank	250			
	Total	450		**Total**	450
1 Feb	Balance b/d	450			

Rental income

Date 20XX	Details	Amount £	Date 20XX	Details	Amount £
31 Jan	Balance c/d	1,000	01 Jan	Balance b/f	400
			28 Jan	Bank	600
	Total	1,000		**Total**	1,000
			1 Feb	Balance b/d	1,000

ALER

36   SMITH & SON

A E   L R

Account name	Amount £	Debit £	Credit £
Fixtures and fittings A	8,250	8,250	
Capital L	18,400		18,400
Bank overdraft L	4,870		4,870
Petty cash control A	350	350	
Sales ledger control (SLCA) A	42,870	42,870	
Purchases ledger control (PLCA) L	23,865		23,865
VAT owed to tax authorities L	10,245		10,245
Inventory A	9,870	9,870	
Loan from bank L	22,484		22,484
Sales R	180,264		180,264
Sales returns R R	5,420	5,420	
Purchases E	129,030	129,030	
Purchases returns R E	2,678		2,678
Discount allowed E	2,222	2,222	
Discount received R	3,432		3,432
Heat and light E	1,490	1,490	
Motor expenses E	2,354	2,354	
Wages E	42,709	42,709	
Rent and rates E	10,600	10,600	
Repairs E	3,020	3,020	
Hotel expenses E	1,890	1,890	
Telephone E	2,220	2,220	
Delivery costs E	1,276	1,276	
Miscellaneous expenses E	2,667	2,667	
Totals	532,476	266,238	266,238

37   EXPIALIDOCIOUS LTD

Account name	Amount £	Debit £	Credit £
Capital	25,360		25,360
Petty cash control	250	250	
Loan from bank	11,600		11,600
Sales ledger control (SLCA)	159,242	159,242	
Purchases ledger control (PLCA)	83,682		83,682
Motor vehicles	35,900	35,900	
Inventory	28,460	28,460	
Bank overdraft	10,063		10,063
VAT owing from tax authorities	15,980	15,980	
Purchases	343,014	343,014	
Purchases returns	1,515		1,515
Wages	56,150	56,150	
Motor expenses	2,950	2,950	
Interest income	400		400
Sales	532,900		532,900
Sales returns	5,760	5,760	
Stationery	1,900	1,900	
Light & heat	6,500	6,500	
Discount received	200		200
Discount allowed	2,160	2,160	
Interest paid on overdraft	550	550	
Travel	1,800	1,800	
Marketing	650	650	
Telephone	1,510	1,510	
Miscellaneous expenses	2,944	2,944	
Totals		665,720	665,720

38   DIXON FURNITURE

Account name		Amount £	Debit £	Credit £
Motor vehicles	A	40,100	40,100	
Capital	L	35,000		35,000
Petty cash control	A	150	150	
Bank balance	A	14,654	14,654	
Wages	E	37,890	37,890	
Travel expenses	E	1,500	1,500	
Rental income	R	1,000		1,000
Sales	R	435,600		435,600
Loan from bank	L	10,000		10,000
Sales ledger control (SLCA)	A	127,456	127,456	
Inventory	A	22,500	22,500	
Purchases ledger control (PLCA)	L	91,250		91,250
VAT due to tax authorities	L	12,500		12,500
Purchases	E	325,600	325,600	
Sales returns	R	6,500	6,500	
Purchases returns	R E	1,250		1,250
Sundry expenses	E	3,600	3,600	
Electricity expense	E	450	450	
Bank interest received	R	360		360
Fuel expense	E	900	900	
Discount received	R	600		600
Discount allowed	E	1,560	1,560	
Advertising	E	300	300	
Telephone	E	1,900	1,900	
Miscellaneous expenses	E	2,500	2,500	
Totals			587,560	587,560

DOCUMENTATION AND RECORDS FOR SUPPLIERS

39   NAN NURSING

Has the correct purchase price of the chocolate puddings been charged on the invoice?	N
Has the correct discount been applied?	Y
What would be the VAT amount charged if the invoice was correct?	£18.00
What would be the total amount charged if the invoice was correct?	£108.00

40   PIXIE PAPERS

Has the correct product been supplied by Pixie Paper?	Y
Has the correct net price been calculated?	N see N1
Has the total invoice price been calculated correctly?	N
What would be the VAT amount charged if the invoice was correct?	£90.00
What would be the total amount charged if the invoice was correct?	£540.00

N1 – the trade discount of 10% should have been deducted so that the net price was £450.

VAT @ 20% on the net price of £450 is then calculated as £90.00.

41   ALPHA LTD

(a)

Purchase return £900

(b)

Invoice 486

(c)

£8,580.00

42   MAXIMUS LTD

(a)

Alpha Ltd
121 Baker St
Newcastle, NE1 7DJ

REMITTANCE ADVICE

To: Maximus Ltd   **Date:** 31 Aug 20XX

Please find attached our cheque in payment of the following amounts.

Invoice number	Credit note number	Amount
864		6,386
	252	964
	258	1,218
	Total amount paid	**4,204**

(b)   A remittance note is for our records only   F

A remittance note is sent to a supplier to advise them of
the amount being paid   T

43   HOLLY LTD

(a)

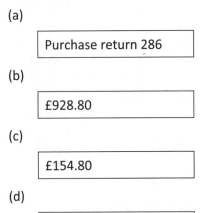

Purchase return 286

(b)

£928.80

(c)

£154.80

(d)

£1,014.80

44   PAINTS R US

Has the correct product been supplied?	Y
Has the correct net price been calculated?	Y
Has the total invoice price been calculated correctly?	N
What would be the VAT amount charged if the invoice was correct?	£30.40
What would be the total amount charged if the invoice was correct?	£190.40

45 EP MANUFACTURERS

(a)

| Cheque for £1,200 |

(b)

| Invoice 488 |

(c)

| £4,850.00 |

46 STANNY LTD

(a)

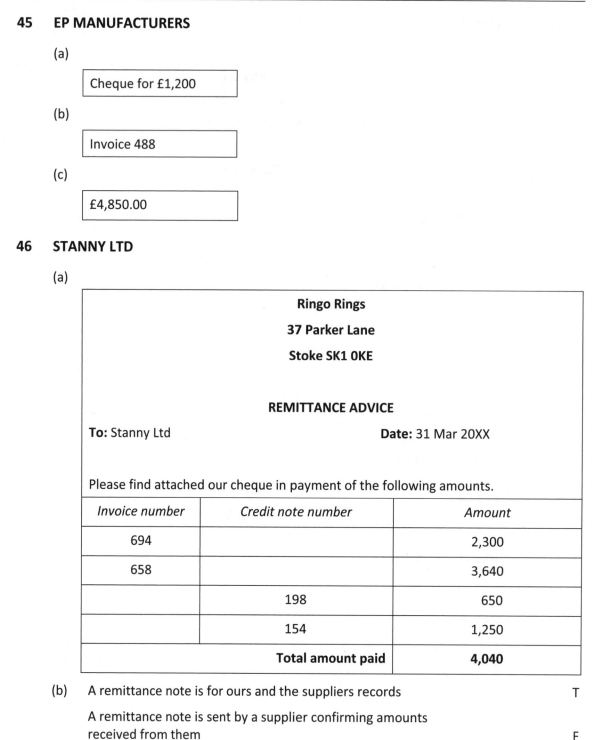

	Ringo Rings	
	37 Parker Lane	
	Stoke SK1 0KE	

REMITTANCE ADVICE

To: Stanny Ltd   **Date:** 31 Mar 20XX

Please find attached our cheque in payment of the following amounts.

Invoice number	Credit note number	Amount
694		2,300
658		3,640
	198	650
	154	1,250
	Total amount paid	**4,040**

(b) A remittance note is for ours and the suppliers records   T

A remittance note is sent by a supplier confirming amounts
received from them   F

47   TOYWORLD

(a)

Cheque for £500

(b)

Invoice 505

(c)

£4,000

48   HENRY HOUSE

(a)

<table>
<tr><td colspan="3" align="center">**Henry House**

22 Nursery Road

Keighley, BD22 7BD

REMITTANCE ADVICE</td></tr>
<tr><td colspan="2">**To:** Abbies Party</td><td>**Date:** 31 Aug 20XX</td></tr>
<tr><td colspan="3">Please find attached our cheque in payment of the following amounts.</td></tr>
<tr><td align="center">*Invoice number*</td><td align="center">*Credit note number*</td><td align="center">*Amount*</td></tr>
<tr><td align="center">242</td><td></td><td align="center">220</td></tr>
<tr><td></td><td align="center">27</td><td align="center">82</td></tr>
<tr><td></td><td></td><td></td></tr>
<tr><td></td><td></td><td></td></tr>
<tr><td></td><td></td><td></td></tr>
<tr><td colspan="2" align="center">**Total amount paid**</td><td align="center">**138**</td></tr>
</table>

(b)   The remittance advice note will be sent to the supplier to advise them of the amount being paid

49 GREY GARAGES

Remittance advice

To: Mulberry Motors

From: Grey Garages

Payment method: BACS   **Date of payment:** 25 July

Items outstanding			Tick if included in payment
Date 20XX	Details	Amount £	
23-Jun	Invoice 213	740	✔
06-Jul	Credit note 14	(120)	✔
13-Jul	Invoice 216	620	✔
19-Jul	Invoice 257	870	
Total amount paid		£1,240	

DOCUMENTATION AND RECORDS FOR CUSTOMERS

50   ALESSANDRO LTD

(a)

Alessandro Ltd

8 Alan Street

Glasgow, G1 7DJ

VAT Registration No. 398 2774 01

Palermo Wholesale   **Customer account code:** AGG42

167 Front St

Stanley

DH8 4TJ

DELIVERY NOTE NUMBER: 24369

Date: 1 Aug 20XX   **Invoice No:** 327

Quantity	Product code	Total list price £	Net amount after discount 12% £	VAT £ 20%	Gross £
40	SB05	2,500	2,200	~~418.00~~ 440	~~2,618~~ 2640

(b)

Settlement discount	110

440

$62.50 \times 40 = 2500$

12% Trade $= (300)$

2200

5% DISC (110)

2090

418

VAT

51   HLB WHOLESALE

(a)

Painting Supplies Ltd

19 Edmund St

Newcastle, NE6 5DJ

VAT Registration No. 402 2958 02

HLB Wholesale   **Customer account code:** HLB24

98 Back St

Consett

DH4 3PD   **Delivery note number:** 46589

Date: 1 Feb 20XX

Invoice No: 298

Quantity	Product code	Total list price £	Net amount after discount £	VAT £	Gross £
20	SD19	300	270	51.84	321.84

(b)

Trade discount

52   MASHED LTD

(a)

Hickory House

22 Nursery Road

Keighley, BD22 7BD

VAT Registration No. 476 1397 02

Mashed Ltd   **Customer account code:** MA87

42 Moorside Court

Ilkley   **Delivery note number:** 472

Leeds, LS29 4PR

                                                   Date: 1 Aug 20XX

Invoice No: 47

Quantity of pots	Product code	Total list price £	Net amount after discount £	VAT £	Gross £
20	P10	100	90	17.28	107.28

(b)

Settlement discount

53   WILLIAM & SAMMY LTD

(a)

Sales invoice 286 ✓

(b)

£4,481.28

(c)

£4,636.88

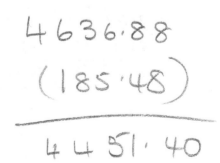

185·48

4636·88

(185·48)

4451·40

54 DIAMONDS & RUBIES LTD

Stavros

121 Baker St

Newcastle, NE1 7DJ

To: Diamonds & Rubies Ltd　　　　　　　　　　**Date:** 31 Aug 20XX

Date 20XX	Details	Transaction amount £	Outstanding amount £
5 Aug	Invoice 3927	4,640	4,640
10 Aug	Credit note 96	980	3,660
21 Aug	Invoice 3964	1,560	5,220
28 Aug	Credit note 104	650	4,570
30 Aug	Cheque received	2,100	2,470

55 MAX LTD

Painting Supplies Ltd

19 Edmund St

Newcastle, NE6 5DJ

To: Max Ltd　　　　　　　　　　**Date:** 28 Feb 20XX

Date 20XX	Details	Transaction amount £	Outstanding amount £
5 Feb	Invoice 4658	2,560	2,560
11 Feb	Invoice 3964	3,290	5,850
21 Feb	Credit note 125	230	5,620
23 Feb	Credit note 139	560	5,060
27 Feb	Cheque received	1,900	3,160

56   BETA BOARDS

<table>
<tr><td colspan="4" align="center">**Beta Boards**
3 Victoria Avenue
Troon
KA5 2BD</td></tr>
<tr><td colspan="2">**To:** Ava Ltd</td><td colspan="2">**Date:** 31 Aug 20XX</td></tr>
<tr><td>*Date*
20XX</td><td>*Details*</td><td>*Transaction amount*
£</td><td>*Outstanding amount*
£</td></tr>
<tr><td>10 Aug</td><td>Invoice 222</td><td>350</td><td>350</td></tr>
<tr><td>12 Aug</td><td>Cheque</td><td>225</td><td>125</td></tr>
<tr><td>15 Aug</td><td>Invoice 305</td><td>744</td><td>869</td></tr>
<tr><td>20 Aug</td><td>Credit note 194</td><td>339</td><td>530</td></tr>
<tr><td>24 Aug</td><td>Cheque</td><td>530</td><td>0</td></tr>
</table>

UNDERSTANDING THE DOUBLE ENTRY SYSTEM

57   ACCOUNTING EQUATION

(a)   Assets less capital is equal to liabilities   True

Assets plus liabilities are equal to capital   False

Capital plus liabilities are equal to assets   True

(b)

Item	Asset or liability?
Inventory	Asset
Machinery	Asset
5 year loan	Liability

58   CLASSIFICATION

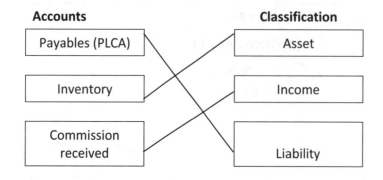

Accounts	Classification
Payables (PLCA)	Asset
Inventory	Income
Commission received	Liability

59   FINANCIAL ACCOUNTING

(a)   Capital is equal to assets plus liabilities   False

Assets less liabilities are equal to capital   True

Liabilities are equal to capital plus assets   False

(b)

Item	Asset or liability?
VAT owed to tax authorities	Liability
Amounts owing to payables	Liability
Money in the bank	Asset

60   CAPEX

Item	Capital income	Revenue income	Capital expenditure	Revenue expenditure
Receipt from sale of motor vehicle	X			
Receipts from credit sales		X		
Purchase of machinery			X	
Payment of electricity bill				X
Purchase of goods for resale				X

61   REVEX

Item	Capital income	Revenue income	Capital expenditure	Revenue expenditure
Receipt from sale of machinery	X			
Payment of telephone bill				X
Purchase of building			X	
Receipts from cash sales		X		
Receipts from credit receivables		X		

62 EXPENDITURE TYPES

Item	Capital expenditure	Revenue expenditure	Capital income	Revenue income
Purchase of a new computer system	X			
Receipts from customers				X
Receipt from sale of fixtures and fittings			X	
Payment of salaries to staff		X		
Purchase of cleaning materials		X		
Receipt of bank interest				X

63 ASSET OR LIABILITY

(a)

Item	Asset or liability?
Factory building	Asset
Money due to suppliers	Liability
Car used in business	Asset

(b) **Complete the sentence below by selecting the correct option to show how this transaction will affect the accounts of ABC Co.**

The expense electricity will *increase*, the asset of bank will *decrease*.

Section 3

MOCK ASSESSMENT QUESTIONS

TASK 1.1

Rocky Ricardo's codes all purchase invoices with a supplier code. A selection of the codes used is given below.

Supplier	Supplier account code
Aldo Ltd	ALD11
Crimes & Co	CRIM12
Diago Delivery	DIA20
Fatima Floral	FAT11
Jim's	JIM09

Purchase invoices and purchase credit notes have been received and partially entered in the day books, as shown below:

Complete the entries in the purchases day book and purchases returns day book by:

- **Selecting the correct supplier account codes from the listing provided above**

- **Insert the appropriate figures to complete the entries**

Purchases day book:

Date 20XX	Details	Supplier account code	Invoice number	Total £	VAT £	Net £	Product 1 £	Product 2 £
31 Dec	Aldo Ltd		213		2,000		10,000	
31 Dec	Crimes & Co		214	2,400				2,000
31 Dec	Jim's		215	960			800	
	Totals						10,800	2,000

Purchases returns day-book

Date 20XX	Details	Supplier account code	Credit note number	Total £	VAT £	Net £	Product 1 £	Product 2 £
31 Dec	Aldo Ltd		275		720	3,600	3,600	
31 Dec	Jim's		8965				400	
	Totals			4,800	800	4,000		

TASK 1.2

The following transactions all took place on 31 December 20XX and have been entered into the sales day book as shown below. No entries have yet been made into the ledger system.

Date 20XX	Details	Invoice number	Total £	VAT £	Net £
31 Dec	Thomas & Son	100	2,400	400	2,000
31 Dec	Johnson & Co	101	4,800	800	4,000
31 Dec	Patrick Wholesale	102	11,520	1,920	9,600
31 Dec	Walker & Wright	103	1,920	320	1,600
	Totals		20,640	3,440	17,200

(a)   **What will be the entries in the sales ledger?**

Select your account name from the following list: Johnson & Co, Patrick Wholesale, Purchases, Purchases ledger control, Purchases returns, Sales, Sales ledger control, Sales returns, VAT, Thomas & Son, Walker & Wright

Sales ledger

Account name	Amount £	Debit ✔	Credit ✔

(b)   **What will be the entries in the general ledger?**

Select your account name from the following list: Bank, Johnson & Co, Patrick Wholesale, Purchases, Purchases ledger control, Purchases returns, Sales, Sales ledger control, Sales returns, VAT, Thomas & Son, Walker & Wright

General ledger

Account name	Amount £	Debit ✔	Credit ✔

TASK 1.3

There are five payments to be entered in Carter's cash-book.

Receipts

Received cash with thanks for goods bought.	Received cash with thanks for goods bought.
From Carter's, a customer without a credit account.	From Carter's, a customer without a credit account.
Net £800	Net £200
VAT £160	VAT £40
Total £960	Total £240
J Pumpkin	*B Row*

Cheque book counterfoils

Lemon Ltd	Remo Motor	Fencer
(Purchase ledger account LEM002)	(no credit account)	(Purchase ledger account FEN001)
£100	£240 including VAT	£600
(**Note:** Have taken £5 settlement discount)		
000123	000124	000125

(a)   Enter the details from the three receipts and three cheque book stubs into the credit side of the cash-book shown below and total each column.

Cash-book – credit side

Details	Discount	Cash	Bank	VAT	Payables	Cash purchases	Motor expenses
Balance b/f			11,450				
J Pumpkin							
B Row							
Lemon Ltd							
Remo Motor							
Fencer							
Total							

There are two cheques from credit customers to be entered in Carter's cash book:

Jeff Jolly   £127 (this customer has taken a £3 discount)

Dolly Darton   £310

(b)   Enter the above details into the debit side of the cash-book and total each column.

Cash book – debit side

Details	Discount	Cash	Bank	Receivables
Balance b/f		1,850		
Jeff Jolly				
Dolly Darton				
Total				

(c)   Using your answers to (a) and (b) above, calculate the cash balance.

£

(d)   Using your answers to (a) and (b) above, calculate the bank balance.

£

(e)   Will the bank balance calculated in (d) above be a debit or credit balance?

Debit/Credit

TASK 1.4

Roger's cash book is both a book of prime entry and part of the double entry bookkeeping system. The following transactions all took place on 31 December and have been entered in the debit side of the cash-book as shown below.

Cash-book – Debit side

Date 20XX	Details	Discounts £	Cash £	Bank £
31 Dec	Balance b/f		200	2,883
31 Dec	TUV Ltd	80		4,000

(a) **What will be the TWO entries in the sales ledger?**

Sales ledger

Account name	Amount £	Debit ✔	Credit ✔

Select your account name from the following list: Balance b/f, Bank, Discounts allowed, Discounts received, Purchases ledger control, Sales ledger control, TUV Ltd

(b) **What will be the THREE entries in the general ledger?**

General ledger

Account name	Amount £	Debit ✔	Credit ✔

Select your account name from the following list: Balance b/f, Bank, Discounts allowed, Discounts received, Purchases ledger control, Sales ledger control, TUV Ltd

The following transactions all took place on 31 December and have been entered in the credit side of the cash-book as shown below. No entries have yet been made in the ledgers.

Cash-book – Credit side

Date 20XX	Details	VAT £	Cash £	Bank £
31 Dec	Entertainment	32		192
31 Dec	Insurance			240

(c)   **What will be the entries in the general ledger?**

General ledger

Account name	Amount £	Debit ✔	Credit ✔

Select your account name from the following list: Bank, Entertainment, Insurance, Office expenses, Purchases ledger control, Sales ledger control, VAT

TASK 1.5

The business maintains a petty cash book as both a book of prime entry and part of the double entry accounting system. The petty cash book has been partly completed for the month of December. The following transactions all took place on 30 June.

Office Supplies paid   £72 including VAT

Postage paid   £10 no VAT

(a)   **Enter the above transactions, in the order in which they are shown, in the petty cash-book below.**

(b)   **Total the petty cash-book and show the balance carried down as at 30th June.**

Select your entries for the 'Details' columns from the following list: Amount, Balance b/d, Balance c/d, Details, Office Supplies, Postage, VAT, Motor expenses

Petty cash-book

Date 20XX	Details	Amount £	Date 20XX	Details	Amount £	VAT £	Postage £	Motor expenses £	Office supplies £
30 Jun	Balance b/f	100.00	30 Jun	Fuel	38.40	6.40		32.00	
30 Jun	Bank	100.00	30 Jun	Office supplies	24.00	4.00			20.00

(c)   **What will be the FIVE entries in the general ledger?**

General ledger

Account name	Amount £	Debit ✔	Credit ✔

Select your account name from the following list: Balance b/f, Balance c/d, Bank, Envelopes, Fuel, Motor expenses, Motor repair, Office supplies, Petty cash-book, Postage, VAT

(d)   **Part way through the month of July, the petty cash account had a balance of £75.00. The cash in the petty cash box was checked and the following notes and coins were present.**

Notes and coins	£
2 × £20 notes	40.00
1 × £5 notes	5.00
11 × £1 coins	11.00
1 × 50p coins	0.50
16 × 10p coins	1.60
10 × 5p coins	0.50

Reconcile the cash amount in the petty cash box with the balance on the petty cash account.

Amount in petty cash box	£
Balance on petty cash account	£
Difference	£

At the end of the month, there was only £2.57 left in the petty cash box.

(e)   **Complete the petty cash reimbursement document below to restore to an imprest amount of £200.00.**

Petty cash reimbursement	
Date: 3.07.XX	
Amount required to restore the cash in the petty cash box.	£

TASK 1.6

Below is a list of balances to be transferred to the trial balance as at 31 December.

Place the figures in the debit or credit column, as appropriate, and total each column.

Account name	Amount £	Debit £	Credit £
Motor vehicles	27,268		
Inventory	18,592		
Bank overdraft	12,333		
Petty cash control	200		
Sales ledger control (SLCA)	169,037		
Purchases ledger control (PLCA)	46,086		
VAT owing to tax authorities (HMRC)	53,376		
Capital	19,364		
Loan from bank	16,413		
Sales	550,064		
Sales returns	38,873		
Purchases	263,387		
Purchases returns	674		
Discount received	1,800		
Discount allowed	2,440		
Wages	152,199		
Motor expenses	2,953		
Stationery	2,450		
Rent and rates	10,345		
Advertising	1,262		
Hotel expenses	1,224		
Telephone	1,599		
Subscriptions	262		
Miscellaneous expenses	8,019		
Totals			

TASK 1.6

TASK 1.7

The account shown below is in the purchases ledger of Rocky Ricardo's. A cheque for £1,000 has now been sent to this supplier.

Coop's Sports

Date 20XX	Details	Amount £	Date 20XX	Details	Amount £
3 Nov	Bank	4,288	1 Nov	Balance b/f	4,288
25 Dec	Purchase returns credit note 102	500	21 Dec	Purchase invoice 123	1,500
			29 Dec	Purchase invoice 189	2,000

(a) **Which item has not been included in the payment?**

Select your account name from the following list: Balance b/f, Purchase invoice 123, Purchase invoice 189, Bank, Purchase returns credit note 102

An invoice has been received from Coop's Sports for £500 plus VAT of £99. A settlement discount of 1% has been offered for payment within 5 days.

(b) **What is the amount Rocky Ricardo's should pay if payment is made within 5 days?**

£

(c) **What is the amount Rocky Ricardo's should pay if payment is NOT made within 5 days?**

£

(d)   A supply of cardboard boxes has been delivered to Rocky Ricardo's by Echo Ltd. The purchase order sent from Rocky Ricardo's, and the invoice from Echo Ltd, are shown below.

Rocky Ricardo

1 Rocky Way

Middleton, M42 5TU

Purchase Order No. RR111

To: Echo Ltd

Date: 7 Dec 20XX

Please supply 1,000 widgets product code 243

Purchase price: £1 per widget, plus VAT

Discount: less 10% trade discount, as agreed

Echo Ltd

2 Walford Way, Essex, ES4 4XX

VAT Registration No. 533 8372 12

Invoice No. 123

Rocky Ricardo

1 Rocky Way

Middleton, M42 5TU

10 Dec 20XX

1,000 .... widgets product code 243 @ £1 each	£1,000.00
VAT	£200.00
Total	£1,200.00

Terms: 30 days net

Check the invoice against the purchase order and answer the following questions.

Has the correct discount been applied?	Yes	No
How much should the trade discount amount to?	£_____	
What would be the VAT amount charged if the invoice was correct?	£_____	

TASK 1.8

On 1 December Rocky Ricardo's delivered the following goods to a credit customer, Alpha Group

<table>
<tr><td colspan="2" align="center">**Rocky Ricardo**
1 Rocky Way
Middleton, M42 5TU</td></tr>
<tr><td>Delivery note No. 2132
01 Dec 20XX</td><td></td></tr>
<tr><td>Alpha Group
Alpha House
Warwick
WR11 5TB</td><td>**Customer account code:** ALP01</td></tr>
<tr><td colspan="2">200 cases of product A, product code A1.</td></tr>
</table>

The list price of the goods was £10 per case plus VAT. Alpha Group are to be given a 10% trade discount and a 2% early settlement discount.

(a)   **Complete the invoice below.**

<table>
<tr><td colspan="3" align="center">**Rocky Ricardo**
1 Rocky Way
Middleton, M42 5TU</td></tr>
<tr><td colspan="3" align="center">VAT Registration No. 298 3827 04</td></tr>
<tr><td>Alpha Group
Alpha House
Warwick
WR11 5TB

Invoice No: 950</td><td></td><td>**Customer account code:**

Delivery note number:

Date: 1 Dec 20XX</td></tr>
</table>

Quantity of cases	Product code	Total list price £	Net amount after discount £	VAT £	Gross £

Rocky Ricardo's offers certain customers a discount, dependent on how much they trade with the business and for how long they have been customers for.

(b)   **What is the name of this type of discount?**

Select your account name from the following list: Bulk discount, Cash discount, Settlement discount, Trade discount

TASK 1.9

The following is a summary of transactions with Bella Pumpkin, a new credit customer.

£1,700 re invoice 1001 of 12 Dec
£2,350 re invoice 1004 of 21 Dec
£940 re credit note 101 of 21 Dec
£470 re invoice 1010 of 27 Dec
Cheque for £2,000 received 29 Dec

(a) **Enter the transactions into the sales ledger of Bella Pumpkin.**

(b) **Insert the balance carried down together with date and details**

(c) **Insert the totals**

(d) **Insert the balance brought down together with date and details**

Bella Pumpkin

Date 20XX	Details	Amount £	Date 20XX	Details	Amount £

(e) **Complete the statement of account below to be sent to Bella Pumpkin**

Rocky Ricardo
1 Rocky Way
Middleton, M42 5TU

To: Bella Pumpkin   **Date:** 31 Dec 20XX

Date 20XX	Details	Transaction amount £	Outstanding amount £

TASK 1.10

(a)   It is important to understand the difference between capital expenditure, revenue expenditure, capital income and revenue income.

Select one option in each instance below to show whether the item will be capital expenditure, revenue expenditure, capital income or revenue income.

Item	Capital expenditure	Revenue expenditure	Capital income	Revenue income
Purchase of computer equipment				
Receipts from credit sales				
Receipt from sale of motor vehicle (non current asset)				
Purchase of motor vehicle				
Purchase of stationery				
Payment of rent				

(b)   **Show whether the following statements are true or false.**

Assets less liabilities are equal to capital	True	False
The business and owner are two separate entities	True	False
A debit increases an item of income	True	False

(c)   **Classify each of the following items as an asset or a liability.**

Item	Asset or liability?
Computer equipment	Select Asset OR Liability
Petty cash	Select Asset OR Liability
Money owed to suppliers	Select Asset OR Liability

Section 4

MOCK ASSESSMENT ANSWERS

TASK 1.1

Purchases day book:

Date 20XX	Details	Supplier account code	Invoice number	Total £	VAT £	Net £	Product 1 £	Product 2 £
31 Dec	Aldo Ltd	ALD11	213	12,000	2,000	10,000	10,000	
31 Dec	Crimes & Co	CRIM12	214	2,400	400	2,000		2,000
31 Dec	Jim's	JIM09	215	960	160	800	800	
	Totals			15,360	2,560	12,800	10,800	2,000

Purchases returns day-book

Date 20XX	Details	Supplier account code	Credit note number	Total £	VAT £	Net £	Product 1 £	Product 2 £
31 Dec	Aldo Ltd	ALD11	275	4,320	720	3,600	3,600	
31 Dec	Jim's	JIM09	8965	480	80	400	400	
	Totals			4,800	800	4,000	4,000	

TASK 1.2

(a) **Sales ledger**

Account name	Amount £	Debit ✔	Credit ✔
Thomas & Son	2,400	✔	
Johnson & Co	4,800	✔	
Patrick Wholesale	11,520	✔	
Walker & Wright	1,920	✔	

(b)   **General ledger**

Account name	Amount £	Debit ✔	Credit ✔
Sales	17,200		✔
VAT	3,440		✔
Sales ledger control	20,640	✔	

TASK 1.3

(a)   **Cash-book – credit side**

Details	Discount	Cash	Bank	VAT	Payables	Cash purchases	Motor expenses
Balance b/f			11,450				
J Pumpkin		960		160		800	
B Row		240		40		200	
Lemon Ltd	5		100		100		
Remo Motor			240	40			200
Fencer			600		600		
Total	5	1,200	12,390	240	700	1,000	200

(b)   **Cash book – debit side**

Details	Discount	Cash	Bank	Receivables
Balance b/f		1,850		
Jeff Jolly	3		127	127
Dolly Darton			310	310
Total	3	1,850	437	437

(c)   £650

(d)   £11,953

(e)   Credit

TASK 1.4

(a) **Sales ledger**

Account name	Amount £	Debit ✔	Credit ✔
TUV Ltd	4,000		✔
TUV Ltd	80		✔

(b) **General ledger**

Account name	Amount £	Debit ✔	Credit ✔
Discounts allowed	80	✔	
Sales ledger control	4,000		✔
Sales ledger control	80		✔

(c) **General ledger**

Account name	Amount £	Debit ✔	Credit ✔
Entertainment	160	✔	
VAT	32	✔	
Insurance	240	✔	

TASK 1.5

(a) – (b)

Petty cash-book

Date 20XX	Details	Amount £	Date 20XX	Details	Amount £	VAT £	Postage £	Motor expenses £	Office supplies £
30 Jun	Balance b/f	100.00	30 Jun	Fuel	38.40	6.40		32.00	
30 Jun	Bank	100.00	30 Jun	Office supplies	24.00	4.00			20.00
			30 Jun	Office supplies	72.00	12.00			60.00
			30 Jun	Postage	10.00		10.00		
				Bal c/d	55.60				
		200.00			200.00	22.40	10.00	32.00	80.00

(c) **General ledger**

Account name	Amount £	Debit ✔	Credit ✔
VAT	22.40	✔	
Postage	10.00	✔	
Motor expenses	32.00	✔	
Office supplies	80.00	✔	
Bank	100.0		✔

(d) Reconcile the cash amount in the petty cash box with the balance on the petty cash account.

Amount in petty cash box	**£58.60**
Balance on petty cash account	**£75.00**
Difference	**£16.40**

At the end of the month, there was only £2.57 left in the petty cash box.

(e) Complete the petty cash reimbursement document below to restore to an imprest amount of £200.00.

Petty cash reimbursement	
Date: 31.07.XX Amount required to restore the cash in the petty cash box.	**£197.43**

TASK 1.6

Account name	Amount £	Debt £	Credit £
Motor vehicles	27,268	27,268	
Inventory	18,592	18,592	
Bank overdraft	12,333		12,333
Petty cash control	200	200	
Sales ledger control (SLCA)	169,037	169,037	
Purchases ledger control (PLCA)	46,086		46,086
VAT owing to tax authorities (HMRC)	53,376		53,376
Capital	19,364		19,364
Loan from bank	16,413		16,413
Sales	550,064		550,064
Sales returns	38,873	38,873	
Purchases	263,387	263,387	
Purchases returns	674		674
Discount received	1,800		1,800
Discount allowed	2,440	2,440	
Wages	152,199	152,199	
Motor expenses	2,953	2,953	
Stationery	2,450	2,450	
Rent and rates	10,345	10,345	
Advertising	1,262	1,262	
Hotel expenses	1,224	1,224	
Telephone	1,599	1,599	
Subscriptions	262	262	
Miscellaneous expenses	8,019	8,019	
Totals		700,110	700,110

TASK 1.7

(a)

Purchase invoice 189

(b)

£594

(c)

£599

(d)

Has the correct discount been applied?	No
How much should the trade discount amount to?	£100
What would be the VAT amount charged if the invoice was correct?	£180

TASK 1.8

(a)

Rocky Ricardo

1 Rocky Way

Middleton, M42 5TU

VAT Registration No. 298 3827 04

Alpha Group

Alpha House

Warwick

WR11 5TB

Customer account code: ALP01

Delivery note number: 2132

Date: 1 Dec 20XX

Invoice No: 950

Quantity of cases	Product code	Total list price £	Net amount after discount £	VAT £	Gross £
200	A1	2,000	1,800	352.80	2,152.80

(b)

Trade discount

TASK 1.9

(a) – (d)

Bella Pumpkin

Date 20XX	Details	Amount £	Date 20XX	Details	Amount £
12 Dec	Invoice 1001	1,700	21 Dec	Credit note 101	940
21 Dec	Invoice 1004	2,350	29 Dec	Cheque rec'd	2,000
27 Dec	Invoice 1010	470	31 Dec	Balance c/d	1,580
		4,520			**4,520**
20XY 1 Jan	Balance b/d	1,580			

(e)

Rocky Ricardo	
1 Rocky Way	
Middleton, M42 5TU	
To: Bella Pumpkin	**Date:** 31 Dec 20XX

Date 20XX	Details	Transaction amount £	Outstanding amount £
12 Dec	Invoice 1001	1,700	1,700
21 Dec	Invoice 1004	2,350	4,050
21 Dec	Credit note 101	940	3,110
27 Dec	Invoice 1010	470	3,580
29 Dec	Cheque	2,000	1,580

TASK 1.10

(a)

Item	Capital expenditure	Revenue expenditure	Capital income	Revenue income
Purchase of computer equipment	✔			
Receipts from credit sales				✔
Receipt from sale of motor vehicle (non current asset)			✔	
Purchase of motor vehicle	✔			
Purchase of stationery		✔		
Payment of rent		✔		

(b)

Assets less liabilities are equal to capital	**True**
The business and owner are two separate entities	**True**
A debit increases an item of income	**False**

(c)

Item	Asset or liability?
Computer equipment	Asset
Petty cash	Asset
Money owed to suppliers	Liability